THROUGH
THE
ROCK

THROUGH THE ROCK

Peter Pegnall

BLACKWATER PRESS

First Published in United Kingdom in 2000 by
Blackwater Press
PO Box 5115, Leicester LE2 8ZD

Printed in England by
Rural Press
Leicester, LE4 5JT

A CIP catalogue record for this book is available from the British library.

ISBN 0 9528557 9 8

Acknowledgements

Some of these poems have appeared in the following publications, to whom thanks are due:

Broken Eggs(Lapwing Press, 1995); Beyond Bedlam(Anvil Press, 1997); Nineties Poetry(Lansdowne Press, 1995 and 1996); The Rat's Mirror(Ha'penny Press, 1999).

Some others have appeared in Agenda, The Big Spoon, Fortnight, The London Magazine and The Transatlantic Review.

Herbert Lomas, James Simmons, Sebastian Barker, Janice Fitzpatrick Simmons, Martin Mooney, Nick Stimson, Peter Dale, Dennis and Rene Greig, Graham Ackroyd, Matthew Sweeney, Medbh McGuckian, Mairtin Crawford, Moniza Alvi, Marion Lomax, David Craig, Bill Herbert, Landeg White and Mahendra Solanki have all offered astute editorial advice and spirited encouragement. I hope the poems themselves are some kind of repayment.

The book is dedicated to Lisa Jones

Contents

Bright Glance

Already in bed. I'll shut my eyes.
nearly. Don't miss a curve, a triangle,
however fast you shed those soft. white things:
it's the sweetest show in town, every night.

As if this weren't enough, when we tumble
or clutch like lovers in a marble frieze,
locked in until the morning, I'll replay
how you bend, unclip, fold away, arch upwards.

Twice over. And twice again. Here you are,
closer than thought, a breathing miracle:
'this is no dream', although delight dreams itself:
image and act soar like dancers, like flame.

A Natural Curriculum

Thomas and Matthew, little devils,
twanging stones at the duck with their catapult;
Matthew's mum lives with Thomas's brother
or Thomas's dad lives with Matthew's mum's mum,
or Matthew's Thomas's brother he says
but a cousin, really, a cousin.

The river Lune scurries over the sandstone
and, once or twice, Matthew's stone scuds the foam
like a missile, like a ballerina.
This is the Devil's Bridge, Kirkby Lonsdale,
there are signs against diving into the Lune,
it is a crime to die here. Thomas and Matthew,
mitchers supreme, devils incarnate,
pocket sized con-merchants.'Will the world end?'
asks Thomas, less pretty, more thoughtful.
'You know, Kosovo and that?' I say 'No,
no, Thomas, no. Live in hope,' I say.

Later, he:'This is very embarrassing.
My brother asked me to ask you for money.
We'd like some pop. Some money for pop.'
It is embarrassing, Thomas. I feel
a pervert. I feel your parent might
drag me to court. I can see that passing face:
"I thought it were a bit odd, a man of his age -"
and even you, ten year old philosopher,
screwing up your eyes as they lead me away,
not saying the thing that might unsay my shame.

For I feel neither shame nor desire, Thomas.
It's new to me, two small boys in caravans,
winter in Newcastle, summer here.
It's new to me, how you love the water,
the shadows, the reeds, the tangled willow,
and how you say 'It's lovely here, lovely.'
You'd never say that if you went to school.

One day, Thomas, I'll learn how you teach me
to speak. Until then, your catapult is true.
Death to the duck. And here's a pound coin: spend it.

The Cows Are Back

The cows are back and I'm so pleased
to see the way they move like warm liquid
the way they hoover the grass,
soak up the rain, shoulder the wind,
nuzzle and chew, nod and shift;
the way their udders swing, their tails trail,
their ears wave like wings.
I love the black and white maps on their coats,
I love to sink in the dark water of their eyes
knowing they know nothing of these things.

I love it when their deep cries
fill the cavern of the day.

Getting Away

A year after his illness. They've bought
the station buffet at Lewes, surprise
travellers with Earl Grey tea, spinach quiche,
potage du jour. Mozart tinkles on tape,
she chats breezily, arranges dried flowers,
half-certain that he's safe in the kitchen.

Broken Eggs

Blake was mad. Clare was mad. Plath was mad. I'm
O.K. at the moment. I don't think crows
slouch like scavenging border guards. That God's
abandoned the game. That, stripped of reason,
we see. If only you'd glimpsed those poor sods
rocking themselves to some dark place who knows
where, dribble gunging their lips, stiff with crime
and refusal, you'd know what fucking treason
spills from intellectuals, hungry to hang
like limpets on those quaking souls who sang
without hope.

And me, too. I'll pound my rhetoric,
grimace to order, take my squashed place
in the hall of mirrors, out on the edge...

The fact is that when your mind flops off track
you might get free enough to fall apart.

And no blazing ladders into the clouds,
no field mice scarcely twitching the long grass,
no small bright wound can put you together,
put you together, put you together
again.

Hunted

I'm on the run. You wouldn't know it. Watch
my eyes, they're watching yours. In Sainsbury's
I act normal. Pile biscuits on bog roll,
nudge my trolley into your legs, fumble
for pen and cheque book. I sign my real name:
clever eh? For five years, invisibly,
MI5 have been closing in. They wait,
like cats in the long grass; my tv feeds them
everything they require, it dreams me.
I've written fifteen letters to Thatcher,
incognito. I'd be at my wits' end
if I wasn't so smart, one jump ahead,
that's me. My brown polyester trousers
merge nicely. I'm too busy for a job;
anyway you can't sit still in this game.
Forget everything I've told you. It's more
than my life's worth; I'd rather you ignored me.

Beatus Ille

I'm a man with a dog and I don't care.
There's a brisk wind and spitting rain and I don't care.
My old mum's got angina and nostalgia and I don't care.
I've lost my boring job and my girl's left
and my best friend's flying to L.A.
and my ankles aren't what they used to be
and I don't, don't care. I'm a man with a dog
and I'll keep walking in this bitter wind
until the bailiff's breaking down the door
and I just can't won't take it any more.

My dog's psoriatic priapic half blind:
he loves sniffing the salt sea and bottoms.

Me too. I'm an incorrigible sniffer
morning noon and midnight. And I don't care
if my pants are yellow and my breath reeks.

I'm dwindled down to the company I keep.

'in a dark time, the eye begins to see'
(Theodore Roethke)

For Eliza

The floor's like ice, the ceiling's squeezing down,
the clock's a liar, the skylark's out of key
you pick your way through jungles in the town

you can't forget that one and one makes three
hear voices mimic voices that you know
you wonder how on earth the prisoner walks free

It's all too crazy true the way you come and go
the way the thistledown cavorts the air
the way you don't know what you only know

the way you dream awake, you burn in falling snow.

November Butterfly

Finer than thread, its legs twine round the dry grass,
there's a last flutter, or is it the wind
flapping a pale brown pair of dead wings?
Hold fast and it looks like you're dancing.

Silent Movies

My next door neighbour's gutter's dripping, splat
splat splat. On the yellow washing line,
a row, a necklace of raindrops. They
catch the light and I think of Andrew Marvell
as I peer close, hoping to see more.
The back yards, the rooftops, the red leaves
how many paintings won't I paint this autumn?
How many moments skim across like
a riderless scooter, like a Martian on a quick trip
to the blue planet. To the place where they all
run like Buster Keaton in Big Trouble,
their eyes brimming with panic and self-pity.

This is where I live, But I long for elsewhere;
oh, not the quick dive downwards, nor some evening
in Siena, not really. Call it a stillness,
a place too private to wrap in words,
but only words can get you there, maybe.

I'll do almost anything to avoid
reflection, A friend, a sixty year old women
glimpses a witch in shop windows. Bad enough,
but what if you catch your mind unawares?
Won't you spin and spin like Rumplestiltkin,
or as usual, will nothing happen and
you'll still be around, scratching the earth
for something to do. And something to do
with that. As my hippy pals used to say
PAY ATTENTION. You can hear the grass grow.
It made sense as long as you didn't ask why?

'all of us are rain under rain' (Pablo Neruda)

i.m. Ricardo Corvolan, 1965-1999

I think of you in doorways. Orange t-shirt,
a bottle of beer, five o'clock shadow,
coiled for action, argument, laughter.
Nothing in you seemed to lag behind.

I'm sure you smelt sex in the summer morning,
in the creamy curves of the honeysuckle,
in the buzzing grass, in the plump chestnut trees;
gently does it, like a tongue of water.

Your heroes aimed paper missiles, sang war-cries
savage as healing, louder than death, sweet
as surrender. You'd cut off your hands,
drink paraquat, kill, sooner than bend your knees.

Did you eat ashes? Was there no blood-red wine
to hand, no friendly cushioning thighs, no word
from the boys? *Come out to play, Ricardo,*
yesterday's news only repeats itself..

And how could you think there's no tomorrow?
When you cupped that swallow hard in your palms,
carried it to the church door, flung it high
and free, watched it scissor the blue velvet,
did you fly yourself, even for a second?
Did you sense flight, as you stood in that doorway?
I shall make much of the earth in your absence,
Ricardo, your taste for fruit, wine, flesh and sky.

Knitting Spaghetti: Fourteen Sonnets.

1.

I'm so tired of saying how tired I am
how irked and cornered by what I've chosen
torn and terrified alone, frozen
in company. What would you think of a man
garrulous as water, closed as a clam,
nostalgic for 'yes' plunged into 'no' -then-
all swagger and wisecrack, profile and posing
cracking in pieces to a silenced plan?
Begin at the end. This is a project
to waken the dead, a resurrection
of nothing less than a person, self-wrecked,
writhing inside his glassy reflection.
This is a waste of paper, a gust of wind
fourteen times fourteen, screwed up in the bin.

2.

Picture him, at a desk in an emptied room,
his 'good with children' child like face crumpled,
his fingers drumming out a ticktock gloom -
all motivation gone. He's been rumbled,
at least the loudest voice announces this
the one that's forgotten how to speak.
The best of nights to come are nights half-pissed
the best of days another wasted week.
What is it that fixes the smile, bolts back
the shameful cry? How long before routine
capsizes, slides under the slackened
will? This is no drama, this is the scene
where pretend goes naked for the waiting crowd
"I can't go on" dumbshows inside the cloud.

3.

Leave of absence: ill-wishers, well-wishers
on hold. Tablets lined up like promises,
'know yourself' paperbacks, hot air and pressure
his baffled child confined to morning kisses,
night time stories. Making a life without
a name, without a having to be there:
a table for one, a mouthful of doubt,
a leftover panic. Learning to care
as if by choice or chance, the happy way
a world turns. Hours of unremarkable grief,
painting by numbers: grey on grey on grey-
a splash of confession for no relief.
And all the while the friendly loss of face
icy nostalgia, that sometime singing place.

4.

Try art galleries. Too many words, Peter
let your eyes relieve that restless wrangling
know that there's silence, somewhere sweeter:
a woman's back, a willow dangling
in water. Grieve for what you can't know,
how long you'll be like this. How to go on,
how to hold the hurt in, how to let go,
how to keep her love, although you've gone
and don't know when you'll be coming home.
Try landscape. Plant yourself on the hillside,
be a tree of patience, make your own room
where goats graze and silver herons glide.
Imitate happiness. Nothing better
to do; go and write your next last letter.

5.

Now you're here. Good morning, Iberia,
the cockerels screech your name: *Peter Pegnall,*
Peter Pegnall, eight hundred miles nearer
the same guilt. But taste the blue, the sweet smell,
white walls, skinny dogs, a woman in black
creeping along the dirt road. Not belong.
Here. Me. Last night I dreamt of going back,
a smatter of Hounslow, a Dylan song
a sharp figure who knew what he wanted
much loved in dance hall, arts centre, her bed.
As the sun announced itself, as the haunted
whoever it is hauled my body legs head
into a bright Algarve morning, beware,
liar on the loose, stare through his practised stare.

6.

Dance dance dance, he said, as if I knew how,
as if I could swish around cool as Bogart,
skate carelessly on the thin ice of now,
tap suave patterns on the floor. I can't start,
you see, I'm netted by this legacy
one step sideways, backwards, skip then stumble,
my head and limbs and body don't agree.
And if the dance is metaphor, I fumble
for a sentence I know I can finish
for a 'complete thought' I can call my own.
Like an over fed dog, like a landed fish,
like a sometime soccer star on loan
to Doncaster Rovers, there's no more movement:

lie low; tell no-one; pray for improvement.

7.

A flutter. While the sun god grills the earth,
while sparrows tumble and squeak, while my shirts kick
and billow on the line, it's all birth
and brightness, it's forever held so quick
it disappears. Beneath the flutter, what
next? Where to? If only this were enough
the deep unknowingness of ripe and rot,
the glad accepting brave it out or bluff.
Yesterday, pasting her mobile to her cheek,
a pink English woman seized the time:
'It's a great, glorious glitter, I can't speak
for how lovely it's been.' I knew I'd rhyme
this company I keep. Like her, my words
never fail to fail again, clasp air, bleat like birds.

8.

Gouge it out with your nib, tap it on the screen,
be your own couch, your own listening ear,
your own sharp angled 'yes' to what you mean to mean,
however ugly. Get on first names with fear,
with rage and grief withheld, cascaded,
shell off your sorry, your *thank you all the same*
crawl inside a past that drank you, raid it
for its knives of no, its play up, play the game,
its grin and bear it. Wave your arms, conduct
pizzicato trembles in the morning blue,
outface the silver, a smile safely tucked
in your poised armoury. At this moment, you
were you alone. All your other figures
line up for inspection, bigger and bigger.

9.

For god's sake pack it in, or pack it tight,
get a cartoon grip on family demons:
picture the breathless fumble in the night,
the stench of promise, subterfuge and semen
the bloom of paper roses on the wall,
majesty of spiders on the ceiling,
the price she paid when kindness came to call,
and though it's rape divorcing sex from feeling
it's worse than that stage-managing the facts
to serve that special sense of child abandoned,
to write a birthday message smeared and cracked,
reporting half-remembered pain at random.
Be satisfied with this and nothing more:
she knew no better on the borrowed floor.

10.

Might as well talk to yourself. Go ahead,
play with your private parts, it's the big event,
mumble disconnections, repeat what you've read
or garbled. All your golden words were lent,
the weight of history spangles your ignorance
brackets your collapse. A boy with an odd stare
fostered by Richmal Crompton, D.H. Lawrence,
chirping off-key, wonky eye and curly hair,
Bob Dylan clown-prince of your would-be antics
your dark side of the coffee bar blues.
(Who could forget your wrestle with semantics,
your gypsy enigma, your snakeskin shoes?)
Drink it all in, veined somewhere in middle age,
too fat to tango, too choked to leave the stage.

11.

Getting bleary eyed's one thing. Believing
as if you'd carved in stone, as if your dead dad
spelt out the way to forge ahead, inweaving
truth and flux, that's another - self pity clad
in self portrait. What a creepy thing to do,
under the shadows of a racing cloud,
next to the glitter of a marine blue,
draping your daytime in a conscious shroud.
Put it this way, it's possible to breathe,
to pass the thin wafer of love without
absolute perjury. To know how to leave
as if your coming back's not held in doubt.
Shoulder your burden, get back up the hill:
you move slightly onwards, just to stand still.

12.

Or find another arse to sniff. Relish
nausea, scan the town for mobile phones,
laptop maestros, the satellite dish
on the Georgian apartment. Never alone
with a sneer, glued to the 'me generation'
the 'I'll do it my way with feeling' brigade,
glad to despise a therapy nation
coddled in victimhood, making the grade;
convince yourself you glide untainted,
conserving all that truth you have to offer -
a touch of the satirist, the sainted,
the fool. And all the better that grating cough,
these fraying trousers, the once attractive
whisky frown. Unhappy, that's the way to live.

13.

Come off it, now. Affectation winds through
the dark passages, goes only so far,
too far. Enter the look-alike, on cue,
aphasic, abashed, displaying his scars,
incurious. Outside, the lawn grows to seed,
slugs munch the marigolds, the light looks in.
And what is it dissatisfaction needs,
to what end this alphabetic skin,
this cormorant gloom? As Tony Hancock
might have said 'What does it all mean, eh?'
daydreaming his way through suburban wreck,
twisted reflection. This is where you stay,
like it or not, this is what you've made, ruined,
knitting spaghetti, spelling out the wind.

14.

Like a glimpse of Hitchcock, like a splatter
of Tarantino, you must have noticed
my signature. It's the style that matters,
a gape of caesura, a flick of the wrist,
a voice like black coffee in the morning;
come to me undressed, I'll drape words across
our shame, I'll scream all the too late warnings
as we squash like hedgehogs. Now I'm the boss,
I'd prefer my lexicon to catch fire,
my steady pace to stumble, my fantasy
to rummage through the secrets of desire
spit milky skeins of undigested me.
Breaking it down, there's nothing left to mend:
one-handed couplet, as if it were the end.

Dog, Man, President, Dog

All snout and tongue and dark blue dangling bollocks.
he needed me to run away from, wait for:
his sudden dashes into the sandhills
pausing only to squeeze a little piss
across the dust. Once, he squirted yellow
on the white walls of Presidente Soares'
summer palace. The fat guards shifted eyes
form dog to man, man to dog. Indolence,
not the army, secures the state. Beach shorts,
a straw hat, t-shirt - these the bright robes
of Portugal's suave administrator.

Good luck to him. And to that ambling dog,
who doesn't grow impatient as I muse,
who bounds gleefully to my thin whistle,
who has learnt to avoid the mad drivers,
who refuses meat from a stranger's hand.

Splendid, this difference between us all.

Fred Astaire

Describing arcs and circles in the air,
black snakes around a malacca cane: your face
like a silly skull, your voice thin, tremulous,
you glide amongst triangles of white tulle,
effortless perfection, draining every
current of yourself. Like plating the fool,
like composing a souffle, you capture
happy victims. Sidewalks, subways, trash cans
painted glorious colours by your feet....
Even bed sitting rooms dance in the corner -
farewell arthritis! So long varicose veins!
a star flickers, who cares about screenplay?

Why did they display you near death, a weak,
broken dolly, scarcely able to speak?

In the Pink: Nude Bathing at Brighton

A librarian, he shelves his week-day
self and gets his clobber off. Dangle, strut,
picking his way along the pebbles. Tubes
and flat cushions of flesh sprout along the shoreline.
Be naked and free! If only he'd come
before; this might have been the life he's missed:
forty-five; bald; a mouth you'd never kiss.

First Love.

Springing tiptoe up the stairs, she wound the thread
to her room. We passed a tv, cracks of light,
a voice on the phone. Squeezed in a single bed
we fumbled and fitted, not quite, all night.

5 a.m. on the streets of Holland Park
my smelly fingers a secret prize,
a fire in the sun, on song with the lark:
the milkman saluting her stars in my eyes.

Stranger

I've watched it fall in two full days,
lounging in a wicker chair in Westchester,
my friend's fine white slatted house settled high
under beech and birch and pine. His dog skoots
and circles, spraying leaves like laughter.
It's as nearly nothing to do as I can find,
schooled in up-to my eyes anxiety,
perfectly out of tune with the forest.

And yet I like it here, I like away,
I like making no difference.
Pacing New York's gulping immensities,
jumping high to be heard, I mouthe 'what the fuck?'
as the jaws of the city grind and grind
and still there's not enough. Someone's banished
the sky, you'll have to glare like headlights,
bulldoze or be bulldozed. This is a show
with ten million scripts, a caterwaul of egos,
an imperative of walk on bys.
Panhandlers sing their stories, drip their tears;
love the city and be swallowed,
as its glass eyes glare down from dead sentries
forever presenting arms to the future.

So I'm happy in leafy affluence,
where the only chase is a runaway dog,
teasing out from the neighbour's willow tree:
the only choice Irish or Scotch and when?
Me for the musty flakes of autumn,
tall trees with roots in the earth, dances
in a changing sky, a glow that darkens.
If you don't belong, belong here.

Crusaders

Let me get this straight. We're *downgrading* a cheat,
a liar, a man who bamboozles the law,
a man who holds his people in contempt,
who would do anything to cling to power.

We're compelled to release the poor fools in his grip
by bombing them. We'll spirit away
his weapons of mass destruction with weapons
of mass destruction. He consults no one.
He diverts attention from his own crimes
with crimes so spectacular the gods weep.

The Christian God weeps. Now is the time for love,
or just a snatched moment in a White House.
Is there anywhere for the Christ child to sleep?
Is there a place where Herod won't swoop like an eagle?

Or will Herod tear Herod until
there's no more morning, no more night, only
men in boiler suits, white hats, rubber gloves,
fumbling the rubble for torn flesh, raw bone?

A Late Lunch With The Master

As he spoke of poetry, his own,
I couldn't help but see the statue,
a naked body, larger than life,
at his shoulder. From his ear grew a penis,
stocky, pendulous, crowned with clay curls,
a fountain of inspiration.
I drank in the praise, offered my own mouth.

I can't recall if he was the 'clouds parting'
or if he 'dived into the darkness'...
either way the world's only just wide enough,
his orbit the upper air, a golden past.
My hired car bounced me home, just in time
for the real sun to sink like a snooker ball,
a baseball cap, a painted nail, a wish.

The Ambassador Sauna is now a Caring Lady Funeral Director

It's all horizontal now. No feather light
fingers, no white lace "who's a naughty boy?"
thonged to the bedstead. Not a flicker.
These softened voices keep you in the cold.

And yet the smiles could be the same, the welcome,
the velvet cushions, the pastel tissues,
the paraphernalia of shared secrets,
incandescent loneliness. 'A nice send off.'

A moment's splatter of semen. Adjust
your dress and get on with it. What you held
you imagined, a little winter love.
Pad across the pink carpet into the careless outside.

Through the Rock

Your love clings like candy floss on my lips;
I'm on the ghost train, alone, in winter.

I can see you on Sunday afternoon,
frightened. Cleaning the car like a disease.

I'm sweet and brittle. The greeting runs through
my stick of rock: fuck you for having me.

Stardust

She lingers by the rain spattered window,
gazing blankly into a bright city:
inside, fusty hallways, voices fading
behind closed doors, her own, echoing room.
Almost afraid to move, she lifts the phone
and lets the purr dangle from her hand;
the plastic clunks back on plastic. No one,
Babbling tv's, the shipping forecast,
a child's exhausted whimper, gushing pipes.
Her eyes glint for a few special seconds -
a gulp of gin, a palmful of capsules:
she joins Marilyn in the noiseless night.

Performance

Why do you do this? Piranha faces
poised for the slashing laugh, the lethal yawn:
dark images of inadequacy,
acid imprints of imagined scorn.

Expectation thrills the foyer. Voices,
staccato sharp, clamour and resonate.
Backstage it's chatter or silence, the same
snake pit inside; these last minutes you hate -

but step out and let fly, your parachute
a tattered rag, yourself, the searchlights rake
the chill sky above a terrified town -
and still you sing, and still the house comes down.

Bertram

A breath of wind might blow him over:
he's a loose, skinny sack of diseased flesh,
he's letting it eat him sooner than remorse,
he wills death. A cigarette, a glass of port,
the clamour of hidden, theatrical grief.
He has no other company, but for
'that impossible dream of being an artist.'

By his own account, his portraits disturbed,
horribly lonely, contorted. People don't buy
but love his flowers: Jacaranda, borage,
they can't see the twisted veins, the torn stems.
I hate to think of the chaos in his home,
hate to stand too near the flavour of torment,
the sheer fall of death. Some angel lighten his going.

Barbecue

for Janice

Last summer I flexed my handyman skills,
forced nuts into bolts through shoddy tin sheets,
scrambled for washers on the dusty stones,
started over, squinting at Japanese English.

1 was not alone in this primeval
mystery. James Simmons, screwdriver supreme,
bent and grafted at my shoulder. Poets
know when to turn their hands to simple tasks.

Women poets more so: from the kitchen,
Janice egged on our manhood: 'You'll never do it!'
Pyramids of fat sausages, chunky chops,
salads fringed with basil, starlit with borage.

The wheels might have been a touch rickety,
there was something, who knows what, left over,
the odd unbolted hole. But the fire was lit,
the charcoal glowed, the evening sang with flavours.

This may-time I cheated, bought a ready-made,
sipped whisky as I prodded the chicken,
looked across the hazy, heavenly Yorkshire Moors,
miles and months from Donegal, but right there,

right there, children playing safe in their back yard,
busy doing nothing but be alive.

You Don't Have To Stay Forever

We love each other best when we're leaving,
I to the pub, You almost anywhere:
parting grins and kisses aren't deceiving,
it's just the way neurotics learn to care.

Disinheritance

The streets of Hounslow sparkle in winter,
frosty grey slabs, patterns to skip across.
Nowhere to live, really, bricked with small fears,
acceptance. Go shopping when you can't stay in.

Fat women, fatter men, ugly children
snivelling. Teenagers slouch like empty coats.
The pubs are stuffed with refugees at home,
telling short stories, as far as they go.

I could ride my bike across stubbled fields,
I could scrump apples with my friend Timmy,
I could take root in the park, girl-gazing.
A real boy, snot-sticky, alone at night.

And that's what I can't reach. Did I tremble
or shriek? Or was I warm when light faded
and were the voices downstairs promises
they'd keep? What are dreams worth in Hounslow?

You're not Winston Churchill, you're not a girl,
you're not a weary detective. Peter.
Peter, like a pixie with a bad eye,
Peter, hug him tight, poor little Peter.

I hate you. You never come when I call,
you're always getting me wrong. Stop laughing.
I love the girl on the train, her white socks,
her neat hair. She loves me too, I can tell.

The thing is, can you live? Accumulate
experience like coins, it tumbles, slides,
slips away. The world's no theatre, but act,
you're on, you were then, behind the curtain.

It's hard to describe who you are. A child
says 'me' like an object, trying to hold on.
And a voice still happens to you, like breath
you don't intend, can only hear at night.

I want that little boy, he's hiding now
like he did with Fiona, under the bed
kissing and kissing. How could he climb out,
blink in the full glare of his family?

And is that it? Saying 'no, I didn't,
you've got the wrong man, I was just passing
and feeling that way. None of it's true now.'
If you believe your story, tell me, how?

West Pier Romance

Tonight the West Pier floated into the sea,
glowing like a Christmas tree in Norway:
some of us danced for the first and last time,
reckless and graceful. The moon smiled, the stars
singled out shy lovers risking fingers,
folding like velvet. Saxophones gargled
nostalgia, it was Scott Fitzgerald, it
was a Monet in your auntie's attic

There's a pink grapefruit on the horizon,
it's five-thirty and cars are ironed out
along the coast road. The pier's crumbling fast,
but you can dream can't you? Like a sad captain
skimming his wheel chair past the winoes
and the silent bandstand, I remember
things that never happened. Waltzing in the wind.

Dave's Dad

Dave's dad played gypsy violin:
kebabs by candlelight, love songs
squealing in a Soho cafe;
long, black hair flopped in greaselets,
his giant nose danced through the smoke.

He'd gabble crazed philosophy,
sucking tea from a grubby mug:
we'd share cigarettes and despair
in a small front room in Shepherd's Bush,
stinking of damp and dope and cat's flux.

The young girls he chased all escaped,
like his wife years before. Dave stayed,
long enough to find the first one
who'd say yes. His dad sank slowly,
clutching a book of Zen and a plastic rose.

Ophelia in the Living Room

It's a rich and sickening story. She died
making no sense out of it, dressing up
to go under. Much too easy for us,
picturing despair, sharing what went wrong,
turning away as if that were enough.
She slipped free, simply couldn't face it,
gathered flowers like a little girl, clutched
the cold air, sang snatches of old songs, cracked
the world in a still green looking glass. Men
blame themselves by striking attitudes.

Our lives continue, headaches, small worries
closing in like china dogs. Tragedy
happens elsewhere, under blood-red skies,
in books, rooms we'll never quite enter. No.
This is it, nothing more special to come;
you scream and I babble half-excuses,
numb with disbelief. What did you expect?
Cliches fit close, like goose pimpled skin.

And, yes, the girl defined herself in death;
misused by her daddy and her lover,
all three remembered that way. As she zig-zagged
towards the water, did she feel each step,
know exactly where she was going?

In Place of Prayer

It's always too early. Thomas and Martha,
drowned at play in the Severn's wide waters,
they held tight and lugged each other down.
Leaving the world, they changed it, they remain:
not all the seas swallow one moment's grief.

But call them by name, those unformed faces;
like small fingernails piercing our palms they grip,
they plunge us deeper than memory, we choke
on borrowed words. Death separates the living;
each new funeral rehearses the last.

Jamie smashed through a shop window, bled white
as his motorbike throbbed. Fourteen years old -
too young by far, too old to be an angel;
stopped dead; a church swelled with children's voices,
his young sister's face set in silent rage.

I lack ceremony. How shall I let go?
This year one more 'accident'. A girl, Robyn,
crumpled like a paper doll. The next world
mocks this one. O pray for the living,
make shapes we can see in the gathering dark.

Flatmates

I'm down here punishing my typewriter:
one more article for Gardeners' Monthly -
'Hardly Hedgerows: Fir Trees in the Suburbs.'
It's November and the sky's yellow,
the city shrivels, there's no promise
in the air. This ancient machine
marches like a bailiff through my poverty.

Upstairs I can't hear a couple making love,
can't guess their sly caresses, whispered lies,
don't imagine they hear me on the job,
how they pity me. Listen as I pace and sigh.
Perhaps I'll move. Buy an Amstrad,
Swap my square of concrete for a square of green.

Somewhere outside the window. Somewhere clean.

One Under

Friday the thirteenth, I'm in bed, tin helmet
strapped tight. You'd like my picnic: hard boiled eggs
pickled onions, custard creams, Old Holborn,
a fat bottle of cider. Safe in the fug,
I'll while away the hours, somehow or other.

They're roaring down the road, blind to accident,
avalanche, magpie. Headlight to bumper,
mobile glued to earhole, chasing a tale.
Where will it end? Long live the Dalai Lama,
that's what I don't bother to say to myself.

It started the year Davy went under:
eight fifteen, District Line, Acton Town Station.
I couldn't bring myself to think he meant it -
there was that rainbow of grease, the last three steps,
the driver's face. And blood like a burst pipe.

Saturday. Now there's a thing. Wouldn't you know
it's pissing down, my throat's like gravel
and it's a long heavy haul to the bog.
Best thing I did, buying that answerphone:
'Peter Pegnall's not here at the moment...'

Forbidden Fruit in a Reading Brasserie

What a cliche: a poem to the waitress,
the lovely waitress, the waitress who smiles
at everyone. And makes you feel special
when she smiles like a slice of the sun,
like an orange splash in this grey, tired town.

Tired and grey, oh to imagine better things
as Veronique glides through the dining room,
so many pairs of eyes, of dim sighted eyes
charting her every sway. And what of her silky
southern vowels? A soft Provencal breeze,
a tang of troubadour tales: grief, absence,
the dark castle on the hill, the clown who sings
for dear life. Who can only watch, wonder
and whisper his heartsickness like a password.

This would be a little sad, mais c'est absurde.

Je Ne Sais Rien

After Leon Damas, a free version.

To tell the truth, I know nothing
nothing more noxious
nothing more loathsome
nothing more dismal in the world
than to listen to love
stretching out the long day
repeating love love love
in a low, slow commination.

There was a time
a woman came
a woman came for a while
her arms were loaded with roses.

Fuck This For A Lark

I'm a scarecrow. You don't scare, ignore
my snazzy rags, my outstretched arms. You feed
at will, bounce across the land. I see you soar
and scribble vicious signs over my head.

I cannot crane to see you, cannot read,
cannot do nothing. Rooted here, fruitless,
little children mock and fear me. I'd bleed
now, if I could, whine: 'It's me. Can't you guess?'

Just imagine when you're tucked up at night,
when shrieking winds and bone-soaking fogs assault
the bare corpses, the brown earth, when owls bite
into velvet bodies, when all the bloat

creatures that guzzle and grow in your veins
are rampant and smirking: just imagine
me, dumping my cross, nose pressed to your pane.
Just imagine creeping downstairs: letting me in.

Beginning

I loved you long before. You were the child
marching out of the mirror, making faces
when the world wasn't watching, if you smiled
I climbed inside, warm in secret places.

Where did you go? I looked for you everywhere,
by the lake in winter, by the sea
when the wind whipped my eyes, rain raked my hair,
fell into other arms, found only me.

Between now and then, you slowly appeared,
or I slowly noticed that hollow ache,
echoing all I'd longed for, all I'd feared:
re-learning to love, preparing to break.